The Lighter Side of Jazz

ISBN 0-634-00039-X

EXCLUSIVELY DISTRIBUTED BY

HAL•LEONARD®
CORPORATION
7777 W. BLUEMOUND RD. P.O. BOX 13819 MILWAUKEE, WI 53213

PUBLISHED BY ARRANGEMENT WITH

Music Sales Limited &

Visit Hal Leonard Online at
www.halleonard.com

CONTENTS

CARAVAN
from SOPHISTICATED LADIES

Words and Music by DUKE ELLINGTON,
IRVING MILLS and JUAN TIZOL

5

CHELSEA BRIDGE

Music by BILLY STRAYHORN

DESAFINADO

Original Text by NEWTON MENDONCA
Music by ANTONIO CARLOS JOBIM

Bossa nova tempo

DON'T GET AROUND MUCH ANYMORE

Words and Music by BOB RUSSELL
and DUKE ELLINGTON

EARLY AUTUMN

Music by RALPH BURNS
and WOODY HERMAN

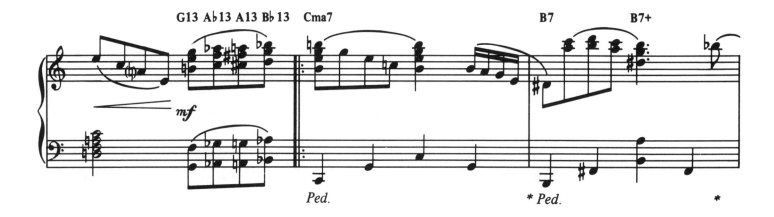

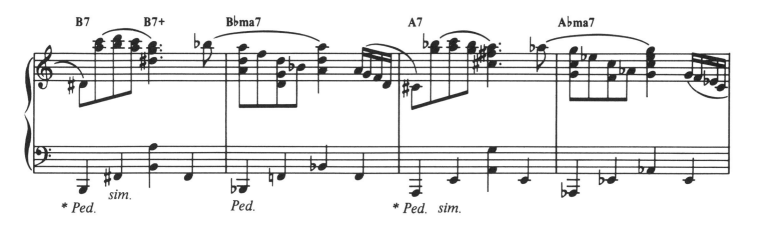

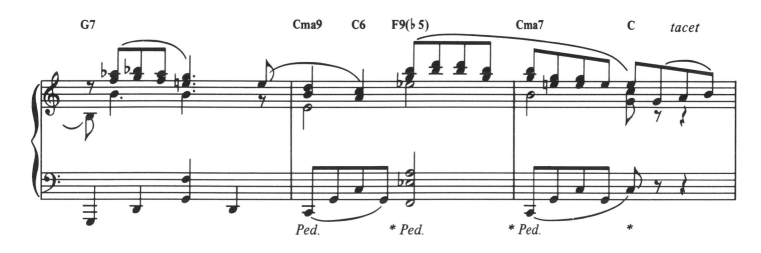

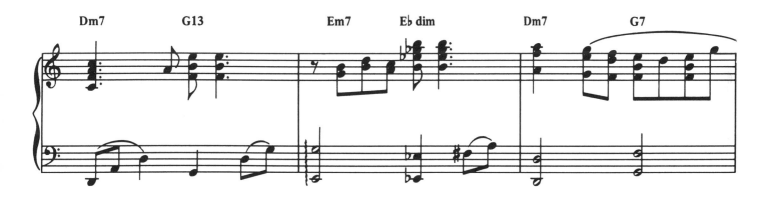

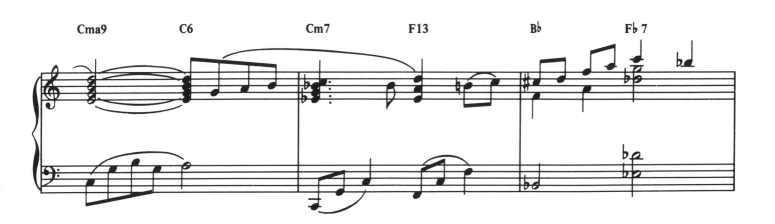

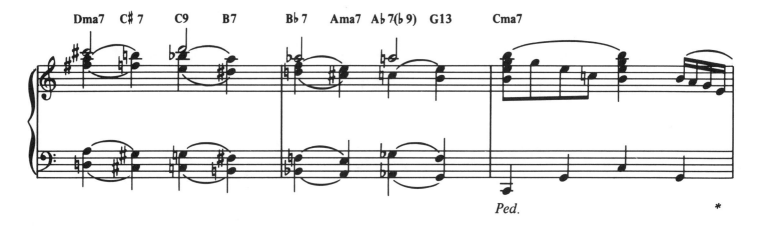

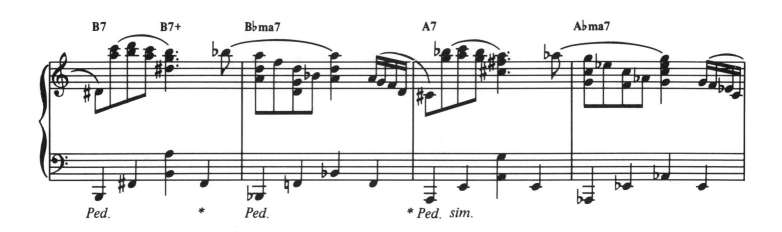

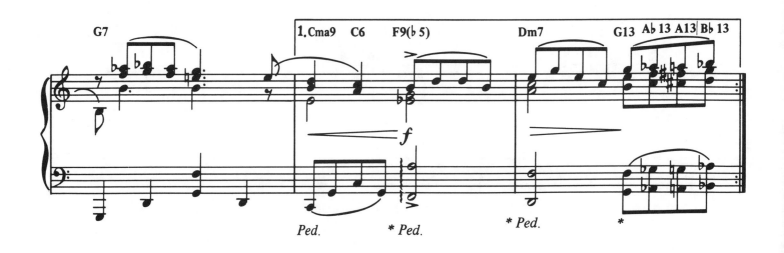

FLY ME TO THE MOON
(IN OTHER WORDS)

Words and Music by
BART HOWARD

HOW INSENSITIVE
(INSENSATEZ)

Original Words by VINICIUS DE MORAES
English Words by NORMAN GIMBEL
Music by ANTONIO CARLOS JOBIM

I'LL BE SEEING YOU
from RIGHT THIS WAY

Lyric by IRVING KAHAL
Music by SAMMY FAIN

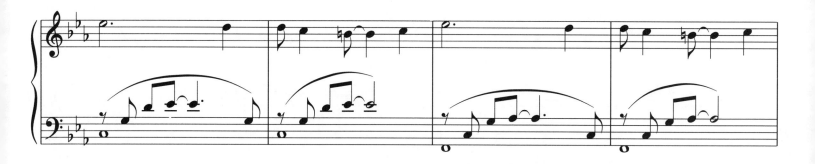

I'LL REMEMBER APRIL

Words and Music by DON RAYE,
GENE DE PAUL and PAT JOHNSON

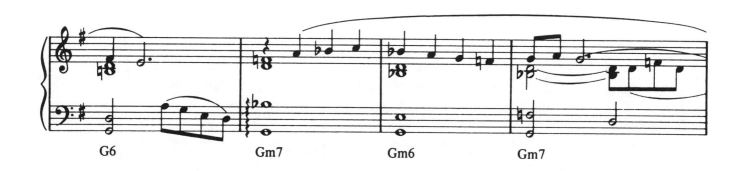

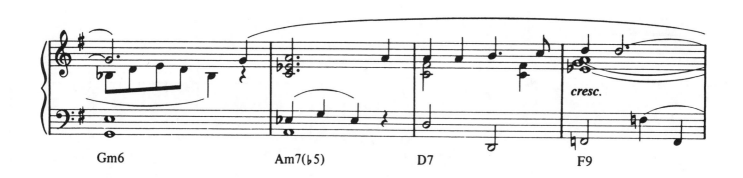

MCA Music Publishing

MANTECA

By DIZZY GILLESPIE, WALTER GIL FULLER
and LUCIANO POZO GONZALES

I'M BEGINNING TO SEE THE LIGHT

Words and Music by DON GEORGE, JOHNNY HODGES,
DUKE ELLINGTON and HARRY JAMES

IN WALKED BUD

By THELONIOUS MONK

ONE NOTE SAMBA
(SAMBA DE UMA NOTA SO)

Original Lyrics by NEWTON MENDONCA
English Lyrics by ANTONIO CARLOS JOBIM
Music by ANTONIO CARLOS JOBIM

Bossa-Nova tempo

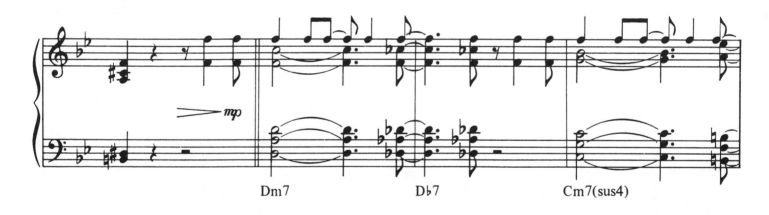

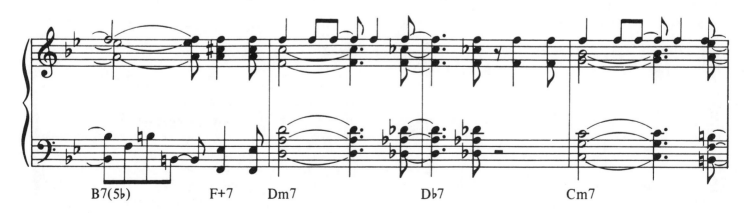

MCA Music Publishing

41

'ROUND MIDNIGHT

Words by BERNIE HANIGHEN
Music by THELONIOUS MONK and COOTIE WILLIAMS

SATIN DOLL
from SOPHISTICATED LADIES

By DUKE ELLINGTON

48

SOPHISTICATED LADY
from SOPHISTICATED LADIES

Words and Music by DUKE ELLINGTON,
IRVING MILLS and MITCHELL PARISH

STORMY WEATHER
(KEEPS RAININ' ALL THE TIME)
from COTTON CLUB PARADE OF 1933

Lyric by TED KOEHLER
Music by HAROLD ARLEN

WAVE

Words and Music by
ANTONIO CARLOS JOBIM

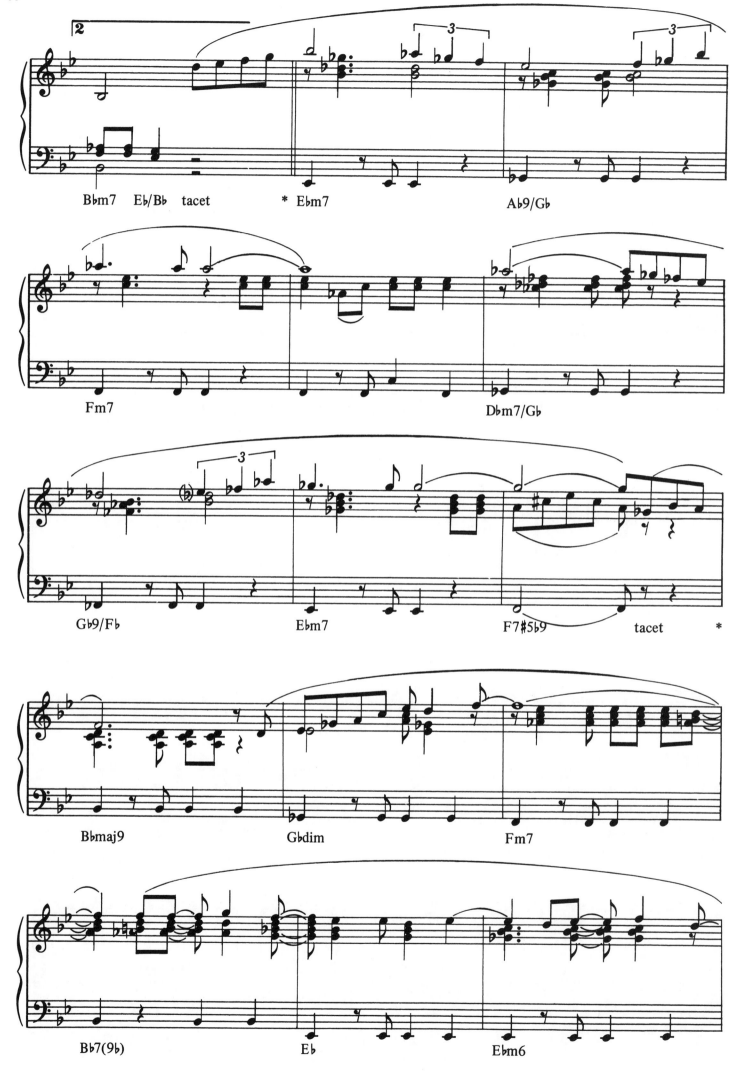

TAKE FIVE

By PAUL DESMOND

TAKE THE "A" TRAIN

Words and Music by
BILLY STRAYHORN

THESE FOOLISH THINGS
(REMIND ME OF YOU)

Words by HOLT MARVELL
Music by JACK STRACHEY and HARRY LINK

UNDECIDED

Words by SID ROBIN
Music by CHARLES SHAVERS

72

73

UNFORGETTABLE

Words and Music by
IRVING GORDON

YOU'VE CHANGED

Words and Music by BILL CAREY
and CARL FISCHER

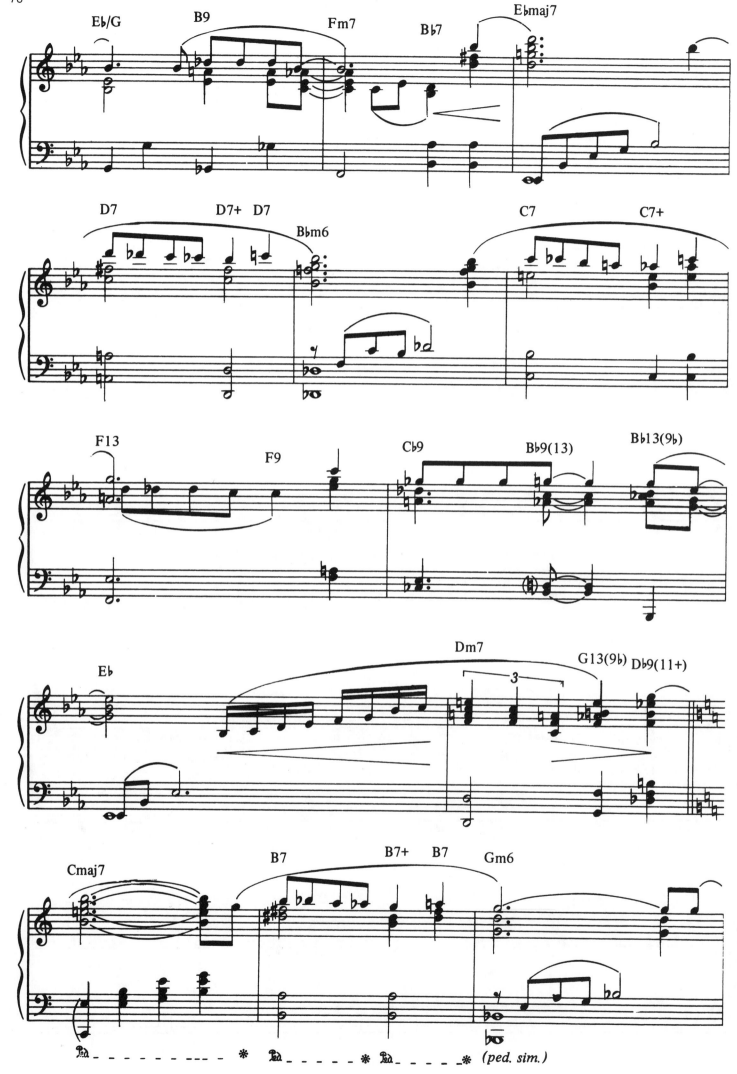